Children
and
Divorce

Roger Smith and John Bradford

National Society/Church House Publishing

National Society/Church House Publishing
Church House
Great Smith Street
London SW1P 3NZ

BV
4463. 65
.S64
1997

ISBN 0 7151 4888 5

Published 1997 by The National Society/Church House
Publishing

Acknowledgement

Prayer (p.60) from the service 'At the Ending of a Marriage'
in *Occasional Celebrations of the Anglican Church of Canada* ©
1992 is published by the Anglican Book Centre, 600 Jarvis
Street, Toronto, Ontario, Canada M47 2J6. Used with per-
mission.

Cover design by Julian Smith

Printed in England by Biddles Ltd, Guildford and King's Lynn

Contents

Contents

Introduction

We live in a time of rapid change. This can pose serious spiritual and ethical challenges, which can be difficult for us to understand or to live through as individuals.

For children and other family members living through separation and divorce, the questions are particularly intense. We know from official figures that divorce rates have been increasing steadily over many decades, with the inevitable consequence that more and more children and young people are affected, and that ever-increasing numbers of families of different types and structures have to come to terms with the consequences of breakdown and reformation. Indeed, most of us are now likely to be affected at some time in our lives, directly or indirectly, by the breakdown of a marriage, or parental separation.

Despite these growing trends, the focus of concern in legislation and policy has been very much on the adults involved in the processes of separation and divorce, and thus, on attributing responsibility by way of seeking grounds for divorce, and coming to formal legal agreements on the allocation of property and assets and incidentally on living arrangements for the children. Recently there has been an encouraging growth in awareness that divorce poses major social, psychological, spiritual and emotional problems for children, which is reflected both in research findings and in gradually changing practices in the fields of childcare and the law. Of particular significance has been the growing emphasis on the use of mediation as a way of focusing adult attention on the needs of their children, and trying to arrive at forward-looking and constructive resolutions of questions relating to the future care of children affected by divorce. This book does not, therefore, focus solely on the enormous challenges which separation and divorce present. It puts forward ideas about how divorce can be handled and the future faced, taking the view that problems, however painful, are there to be solved.

Whilst recognising that enormous changes have taken place, and the challenges that such changes bring, it is important to set change in its context, both spiritual and practical. This will aid understanding of the direction and pace of change, and will help those faced with the consequences of the breakdown of parental relationships to recognise the implications, and to attempt to deal positively with these difficult challenges. Understanding of this kind will, we believe, improve the ability of all of those affected – and this is likely to include most of us at some point in our lives – to respond constructively and supportively to the difficulties faced by children themselves.

This book has distinct purposes:

- It provides a spiritual basis for understanding the issues raised.

- It places trends and developments in divorce in their historic and social context.

- It explores the evidence of the impact of divorce on children.

- It discusses the current legal and political context and, particularly, implications in the light of the Family Law Act 1996.

- It addresses the question of what those affected, whether directly or indirectly, can do with particular reference to the concerns of those who have a role in providing care or support for children.

In seeking to achieve these aims, we hope to provide a deeper understanding of the issues concerned. It is also our intention to provide some ideas about the practical consequences and the way in which constructive answers can be found to further the interests of children affected by the breakdown of their parents' relationships.

PART ONE

Defining the Problem

Chapter 1

What happens when marriages fail?

This is an important but not an easy subject, and we may be helped into it by making a distinction at the outset between the facts of any particular case on the one hand and general orientations on the other.

Orientations about the failure of marriage come in many forms and shapes. They are moulded by such questions as what we ideally desire, what is the moral norm, what is the legal norm, what is the social norm (whether we like it or not) and what is feasible. Things become even more complex when several sets of conflicting norms are involved, for example in a marriage between a Muslim and a Christian, or in a marriage between persons of totally different nationalities.

This chapter is essentially about anchor-points in an Anglican orientation towards divorce.

Although more marriages remain intact than become fractured, and although support for married couples must and should be a proper priority, those whose marriages fail are invariably deeply wounded, and have a real sense of guilt at not having been able to live up to their solemn promises publicly made. It is therefore an important function of the Church to be pastorally resourceful and supportive to those who suffer marital misfortune; adults who receive the care and understanding of their Church at such a time will hopefully then be in a better position to be caring and understanding towards their children, at the time and in the future.

Naturally, the higher an individual's view of marriage, and the more conscientious his or her desire to be a good parent, the more painful and tortuous he or she will find marital failure.

Paradise lost

However, whatever circumstances may arise, no one should allow the existence or the experience of divorce to detract from the beauty and uniqueness of marriage at its best.

Marriage is not the antithesis of divorce, but rather of 'singleness'. It is a most distinctive step forward in personal relationships, whereby a man and a woman freely, lovingly and solemnly give themselves to each other for the rest of their lives. It is therefore celebrated and remembered not only by the couple but by their family and friends as a major milestone in their kinship and friendship network.

In Christian marriage, the attitude of the Church provides a very enriching contribution to understanding its deeper underlying nature and significance. *The Alternative Service Book 1980* (the ASB) of the Church of England portrays marriage in the following ways:

- Marriage is a thoughtfully undertaken lifelong mutual commitment between a man and a woman who love each other, and it is embarked upon formally, publicly and prayerfully (Introduction, p.288, paragraph 4, and Prayer over ring(s), p.292).

- Marriage is a framework for **lifelong security and stability** both for the couple and for any child or children with which they may be blessed (Introduction, p.288, paragraph 3b, and Prayer 26, p.296).

- Marriage is a consecration of the **union of body–mind–spirit** of a particular woman and a particular man which gives a new and special sense of human 'completeness' to each (Introduction, p.288, paragraph 3a, and Statement on gift/reception of ring, p.292).

- Marriage is a special relationship within which the human and spiritual **healing and growth** of each partner can be uniquely fostered by the other (Vows, pp.289, 290).

- Marriage is a microcosm of the relationship of the **closeness, love and trust** which exists between Christ and his Church (Introduction, p.288 paragraph 2).

- Marriage is a relationship which relatives, friends and faith community members have a duty to ensure **is supported**: though without interference or intrusiveness (Introduction, p.288, paragraph 6, and injunction, section 18, p.293).

- Marriage, being a partnership of human love, is, especially if enhanced by the generosity of the love of God, productive of an **outward considerateness and kindheartedness** to family, neighbours and friends (Prayer 3, p.287, and Prayer 27, p.297).

These descriptions show what a high value is placed upon marriage by the Church, and what high expectations of marriage those embarking upon it may justifiably have.

It follows, therefore, that should a marriage – which has been genuinely entered upon with all these hopes and intentions – fail, this is not only tragic for the couple themselves, and especially for their children, but also for their extended family, their friends and faith community.

Human failure: how do marriages fail?

The five most common types of marriage failure are:

(i)   where love between the couple never grows, or where it actually withers and dies;

(ii) where a partner seriously abuses or injures the other, physically or emotionally, and/or a child or children of the family;

(iii) where hearts and minds deeply and dangerously diverge over such fundamental issues as having children;

(iv) where a partner soils or spoils the relationship by an act or acts of infidelity;

(v) where one partner suddenly chooses to desert the other either in extrication from marital commitment or, more commonly, in favour of someone else with whom they may have fallen in love.

In certain cases there may be some combination of these indices of failure.

It should be recognised that while each of these five types of marriage failure offers evidence of marital 'breakdown', the judgment as to whether this is evidence of the final 'death' of the marriage can be taken only by the partners themselves. It may be that both partners are content to live with a loveless marriage. It may be that an injured partner opts to stay with the relationship, seeking to minimise and contain the trauma suffered. It may be that it is believed that some basic attitudes inimical to the relationship may change. It may be that a couple can in some way come to terms with an element of infidelity. It may be that a deserted partner chooses not to close the door on the possibility of rapprochement.

In a Christian Church we have to hold to the view that people have a free conscience – but this does not mean that anything goes. How far a partner or partners will be caring, wise and realistic in assessing whether reconciliation should be pursued or whether or not their marriage is 'dead' will vary widely, and invariably will not be easy. We offer a simple framework for thinking further about this in Chapter 8.

Acting thoughtfully

However, it does not seem unreasonable to suggest that the Church would want a couple on the brink of splitting up to make decisions about this in the same spirit as they entered marriage, viz. not carelessly, lightly or selfishly: but reverently, responsibly and after serious thought. The task for the Church at such a time is therefore to provide space and resources for a person facing serious matrimonial difficulty to arrive at a basic stance and position in a really considered way. It may be a help to such persons to have the opportunity of skilled counselling support. It may be helpful for them to feel supported by intercessory prayer. It may be helpful for them to be able to get away, possibly to a Christian Holiday or Conference Centre, so that they might have time to think of other things or, conversely, to address their problem directly through reflection.

An essential aspect of the Church's debate about divorce, therefore, is for the Church to offer understanding support in such a way that partners of a failing marriage have adequate time, space and understanding friendship in order to reflect upon their options for reconciliation or divorce and to come to a decision about the future in a positive and constructive way. It is crucially important that this process should take place *before* irretrievable breakdown actually happens. If it is true that one marries primarily so that one might serve God and his kingdom the better in that relationship, then the primary purpose of ending a marriage should be to the same end.

Help of this kind by the Church, assisted perhaps by Diocesan and ecumenical resources, will not spare but might even accentuate the feelings of shared sadness when the outcome is the death of the marriage.

Sharing in the loss

It is important for the Church to acknowledge its sadness and to recognise the dimensions of the problems.

1   There will be profound **sadness** for the couple who feel unable to sustain mutual vows prayerfully and publicly made – and for the loss of self-esteem which this will invariably involve for each of them.

2   There will be **concern** for the insecurity and instability which the partners may be experiencing and which any children will certainly be undergoing.

3   There will be a sense of **loss** for a unique partnership between two persons and for the potential of that partnership.

4   There will be **compassion** for a couple who became united in order to help and promote the happiness of the other, and who have subsequently become actually or potentially hurtful and damaging to each other (in one way or another).

5   There will be inner **grief** that a relationship demonstrating the divine work of love and unification has become one exemplifying the human capacity for coldness, or even hate, and for dissolution.

6   There will be **guilt** that more might have been done by congregation members and others to support and encourage the couple in their marriage.

7   There will be **disappointment** that the home created by the married partnership will no longer be able to minister to others in friendship and neighbourliness as it had or might have done.

Concern for the children

Matrimonial breakdown is the particular business of the couple whose marriage partnership has foundered. However, as we have hinted under the second aspect of the sadness of the Church about the breakdown of a marriage, there may well be a child or children to be concerned about, who may be baptised members of the Church of God and equal to everyone else in the household of faith and demanding support and Christian attention.

Here the Church is in a slight pastoral dilemma. For while a partner's determining whether their marriage is open to reconciliation or not is in process, the children are in limbo, hardly knowing any better than anyone else which way the outcome is likely to be. In some cases they may know less than anyone else, because their parents choose not to talk to them about their relationship; because they are unclear what to say; because they do not want their words repeated; because they could not cope with the possible (if not probable) reply; because they think it is none of their child's or children's business.

It should be mentioned that some speak of the loss of divorce as being akin to bereavement. For a child it may well appear worse, because separation from a parent loved and living may be more unclear and difficult to come to terms with than separation from a parent loved and who has died.

Taking a sound position

There are seven firm anchor-points here:

- First, parental honesty and openness (without unnecessary or inappropriate details) with children is always important for their emotional security, self-esteem and understanding of what is going on around them, particularly at such a difficult time.

9

- Second, every possible effort should be made by both parents to show consistency and consideration in the support for and expectations of their child or children during both the crisis and aftermath of a period of domestic turmoil and difficulty. A key requirement is that both parents should continue to be able to pray the prayer to be trustworthy parents (Thanksgiving for the Birth of a Child, section 2, ASB, p.213), whatever the outcome of their matrimonial circumstances.

- Third, where any child involved has been baptised, the availability to that child of his or her godparents for private and trusted discussion could be very valuable indeed. Godparents have a very special function at difficult as well as at happy times in a child's family life. Each child will have their special needs and concerns. (This is discussed more fully in Chapter 6.)

- Fourth, remember that when home life is strained or disrupted, membership of a loving Church community – especially a children's group, youth meeting, uniformed organisation, choir, sport, bell-ringing or other activity – can provide a child or young person with an ongoing anchor and support.

- Fifth, it is essential to appreciate that if the parents are feeling tension and pain about their fragile or ending relationship, and if the Church is sharing in the sadness, how much more must the child or children of the marriage be feeling anxiety, pain and confusion? It is incredible to assume that somehow the children will not notice or be affected in any way. They will have instinctive concerns for their future care. (See also Chapter 3.)

- Sixth, be aware of and responsive to the fact that where cohabiting couples split up, the effects of that separation upon their children is likely to be similar to the effects of divorce.

- Seventh, be aware of the informal ministry of friendship and understanding that a Church member (e.g. a teacher) could give to children or young people of non-Church families who are experiencing deep family unhappiness, and of the wisdom of such persons having the support of a Church group in the exercise of their care and concern.

We should also not forget that where marriages end after, say, thirty years, the children – who are then in their twenties and may have marriages and families of their own – will still feel the pain, hurt and disorientation; some (though not all) would say that they experience it to an even higher degree than if they had been younger.

Chapter 2

Changing patterns
of marriage and divorce

The importance of understanding change

As the previous chapter illustrates, marriage and divorce are bound up with powerful moral, spiritual and political debates. It is important also to retain an awareness of historical trends and developments in order to aid understanding.

Changes in legislation and social behaviour are of considerable significance in the overall picture of marital behaviour and outcomes over the years. A clear understanding of these changes will certainly help us to identify better the continuing human and spiritual needs which arise when relationships break down; and perhaps will also enable us to develop some ideas about the kinds of response and intervention that can be seen as helpful to those affected, and to children in particular. As we shall see, concern for children has not always been accorded its proper priority in approaches to marital breakdown; it is hoped that this is a matter of history, and that the overriding importance of attending to their needs will now be properly recognised.

Marriage and divorce in history

Obviously, marriage in its formal sense has not always been a part of society, and indeed its form and nature still vary considerably around the world. Marriage did not seem to exist, in its formal sense, in ancient civilisations, and at least until the Middle Ages it seems that most marriages among most classes were common-law arrangements.

It was only with the growing influence of the Church that marriage became recognised as a more formal arrangement, which in turn meant that it could not be dissolved except in extreme circumstances. This was a direct consequence of the religious underpinnings of marriage, which implied that it could not be brought to an end by any secular or earthly power.

Timeline

12th century	Marriage embodied in church law. 'Marriage was for life. It came to be regarded as the seat of all social, as well as Christian, virtue.' (Davis and Murch, 1988)
18th century	Act of Parliament still needed to dissolve marriage.
1857	Matrimonial Causes Act: divorce possible without an act of parliament, adultery the sole ground for divorce.
1903	'Nothing is more certain than that . . . the progressive modification of the marriage contract will be continued until it is no more onerous nor irrevocable than any ordinary commercial deed of partnership.' (G.B. Shaw, *Man and Superman*)
1923	Women's rights to petition for divorce extended to equal men's.
1937	Matrimonial Causes Act: grounds for divorce extended to include desertion, cruelty and insanity.

1969	Divorce Reform Act: 'fault'-based grounds for divorce replaced by requirement to demonstrate 'irretrievable breakdown' based on one of the five 'facts':
	(i) adultery;
	(ii) unreasonable behaviour;
	(iii) desertion for at least two years;
	(iv) two years separation by mutual consent;
	(v) five-year separation without consent.
1973	Matrimonial Causes Act: special procedure introduced to allow divorce by consent, but arrangements for children to be subject to scrutiny by judges.
1984	Matrimonial and Family Proceedings Act: further easing of restrictions on availability of divorce and simplification of procedures.
1996	Family Law Act: divorce to be available on application after mandatory period of reflection. Mediation provided for by law for the first time ever.

By around the twelfth century, the law relating to marriage had become integral to church law, and civil law had no part to play in regulating marriage or divorce. Marriage was treated as a lifelong contract, which was not to be dissolved under any circumstances. It was seen as both a social benefit and a Christian virtue, which would help to confirm the social and moral order of society. Clearly, these fundamental assumptions were loosened by the events surrounding the Reformation, and provision was subsequently made for applications to be made to parliament for the dissolution of a marriage.

Partly as a consequence of this, until the mid-nineteenth century, divorce was a lengthy, complicated and costly procedure requiring an act of parliament in each individual case to ratify the ending of the marriage. In other words, there were very few divorces during this period, although it is certain that a much larger number of marriages broke down, or simply ceased to have any real meaning. It was observed by contemporary commentators that second marriages 'without divorce', the birth of children outside marriage, and adultery were all commonplace; the absence of easily available legal routes to divorce does not appear to have guaranteed the stability or sanctity of marriage. It is also worth reminding ourselves that many more marriages would have ended in the early death of one or other partner; indeed, as many marriages came to an end in this way in the 1820s as did by way of divorce in the 1980s.

It was only in 1857 that civil divorce became possible without the passage of a private act of parliament. This legislation achieved two things: firstly, it confirmed that bringing a marriage to an end could be a responsible and respectable course of action. Secondly, it clarified that divorce was no longer simply a matter for the Church, and that the civil law had a clear and explicit responsibility over marital arrangement.

From the time of the 1857 Matrimonial Causes Act, through the succeeding century and a half, there has been a trend towards increasingly less restrictive legislation in the area of divorce, associated with moves towards a more secular view of the marriage bond, and a correspondingly lower emphasis on 'fault' or moral blame as a ground for divorce. These trends, it seems, are partly to do with an increasingly secular society, but are also likely to have been influenced by the upheavals arising from major social change, such as those linked with the two world wars, and periods of mass unemployment. In addition, the changing nature of relationships between men and women, and, more recently, the greater recognition of women's rights, may have had some influence on ideas about marriage and divorce.

The view of the Church

In response to the changes in the social context, the Church itself made a major contribution to the debate in 1966 with its report *Putting Asunder.* This was the product of work undertaken by a group of experts convened by the Archbishop of Canterbury in a context of a growing number of divorces, and increasing concern about the means by which divorces were being obtained. The reliance on fault-based grounds such as adultery meant that such evidence was being contrived in a considerable number of cases, and the law was in danger of falling into disrepute.

The report concluded that fault and moral blame were unhelpful starting-points for the inevitably uncomfortable and adversarial process of seeking a divorce; in any case, the need to prove some form of unacceptable behaviour such as adultery did not prevent those who could afford it from achieving the outcome they wanted. The report sought a much more balanced basis for decisions about divorce, and in particular, drew attention to the need to consider the interests of children more clearly, rather than through a haze of bitterness and recrimination. The report did not, however, favour making divorce easier, because it believed that the ending of a marriage should be subject to real and thorough scrutiny in order to ensure that the relationship had genuinely broken down and was irretrievable.

The fact that the Church appeared to be sanctioning divorce in certain circumstances was one major influence on the growing impetus for reform. Shortly afterwards, the Law

Commission produced its own report, setting out the principles which it believed should underpin the law relating to marriage and divorce:

> (i) to buttress rather than undermine the stability of marriage;
>
> (ii) when, regrettably, marriage has irretrievably broken down, to enable the empty legal shell to be destroyed with the maximum fairness and the minimum bitterness, distress and humiliation.

> (*The Field of Choice*, 1966)

If marriages were to break down, four key issues should be addresssed:

> (a) the need to promote reconciliation;
>
> (b) the prevalence of stable, illicit unions;
>
> (c) injustice to the economically weaker party;
>
> (d) the need to protect children.

The recognition of children's interests is of particular importance as it had not previously been a factor in consideration of the legal issues surrounding divorce.

Breaking with the past

The ensuing legislation, the Divorce Reform Act 1969, accepted the Law Commission's view that marital 'breakdown' should be the basis for granting a divorce, but that this in turn should be subject to proof by virtue of one of five 'facts', including adultery, unreasonable behaviour and separation. However, the intense scrutiny of divorce applications proposed in the Church of England Report was not incorporated in the legislation.

The 1973 Matrimonial Causes Act subsequently underlined the paramountcy of children's interests in divorce proceedings, and under Section 41 included a procedure to ensure that the needs of children were specifically addressed in all cases where they were involved. This principle has since been stengthened by the 1989 Children Act, which has also drawn attention to the need to consider children's wishes and feelings when decisions are made about their future. However, it has also been argued that the simplification of procedures under the 1973 Act, and the removal of certain restrictions such as the three-year bar to divorce under the 1984 Matrimonial and Family Proceedings Act, have combined to make divorce simply a paper exercise, with the result that children's interests are not given proper consideration (Davis and Murch, 1988).

The changing social climate

At the same time as the changes in legal and political contexts, there have been massive shifts in social behaviour which are reflected in analysis of population trends. Since the nineteenth century, there has been a steady and sizeable increase in both the numbers of divorces and the divorce rate (though this has tended to stabilise since the mid 1980s). Thus, from 1912, when less than 1000 petitions for divorce were filed in England and Wales, the increase has been inexorable. In 1993 there were 165,000 divorces; there was actually a slight fall the following year, to 158,000. In parallel with the increase in numbers, the divorce rate has also increased significantly, from three per thousand of the married population in the mid 1960s to 13 per thousand in 1991.

Within this enormous overall increase, there have also been some notable 'blips', such as those occurring after both world wars, and also after the implementation of specific pieces of legislation, such as the 1969 and 1984 acts. Thus, substantial social upheaval and legislative change, appear to have opened the way for the resolution of a large number of pre-existing marital breakdowns by way of divorce. This is a significant observation, because it highlights the importance of distinguishing between marital breakdown and the formal recognition of that breakdown by way of divorce. It is, for example, notable that the proportion of 'separated' lone-parent families declined between 1971 and 1991, while the proportion of the same group of families who were divorced increased over the same period.

These broad trends also disguise a number of other important observations. For example, divorce rates have been found to differ considerably between social classes, with a much lower rate among professional classes than others such as manual workers, the unemployed and the armed forces. Divorce is also more likely where one, or especially both, partners to a marriage have already been divorced. The continuing popularity of marriage means that part of the increase in the divorce rates can be linked to this factor.

Of course, in a very large number of cases, children are involved. It is estimated that around 165,000 children per year are now affected by their parents' (or step-parents') divorce. While it is undeniably true that children have always been affected by marital breakdown, the size of this figure almost demands the development of specific social policy action to respond to the potential consequences.

At the same time as these quite dramatic trends in the field of marriage and divorce have been revealed, wider social developments have also emerged, some of which are clearly linked and which also have implications for policy directed towards children who experience instability and relationship breakdown.

Family structures have recently become both more varied and less stable. While marriage remains popular, the conventional two-parent family with children is now a relatively small proportion of the overall number of households. In addition, because of trends in separation, divorce and remarriage, these families themselves are increasingly likely to experience change. It is estimated that as many as a third of marriages will not survive and one in four children will experience divorce. In addition, children are increasingly likely to be born to lone mothers who are not part of a fixed, secure relationship, or into families whose parents are cohabiting but unmarried.

International change

Because the patterns of living are becoming increasingly diverse, it also becomes more important to develop policies which are sensitive to these variations, and provide effective support to children regardless of their individual circumstances.

Many of these trends are mirrored in other countries, both in Europe where religious differences do not necessarily mean that the trends towards higher divorce rates and changing family structures are greatly different, although baseline figures may be lower; and in other 'commonwealth' countries, where comparisons are almost uncanny. Thus, very similar pictures emerge from Australia, New Zealand and Canada, where in each case the current position is quite similar to that in the UK. In 1994, for example, the divorce rate in Australia was 12.0 per 1000 married persons, while the marriage rate had declined to 38.2 per 1000 persons over the age of 20. In New Zealand the divorce rate in the early 1990s was 12.3 per 1000 married persons, and the marriage rate was 37.4 per 1000 persons over 16 in 1994. In Canada the marriage rate fell steadily to 35.7 per 1000 non-married persons over 15 in 1994. The divorce rate, on the other hand, had risen to 11.1 per 1000 married persons in 1993. In all of these countries, policymakers are grappling with the demands of adapting to changing circumstances and patterns of living.

Changing circumstances, changing practice

While the legislative framework has struggled to keep up with these social developments, changes in practice and attitude among those working with families reflect the need to keep up with what is going on. For example, the legal profession and court processes have been changed to try to take account of the needs of families. Both solicitors and barristers have associations which take a special interest in family law matters, and which seek to develop expertise in these areas. In addition, voluntary bodies such as Relate (formerly The Marriage Guidance Council) have responded positively to new family patterns by seeking to support families and children under stress, whatever the formal characterisation of their relationships. Concern for children is clearly an element in this practice, as it is with those organisations concerned with mediation, probably one of the newest 'professions'. The sheer number of children experiencing separation and divorce has prompted the establishment of more than 60 mediation services, whose aim is to focus specifically on resolving differences between separating couples in order to make effective plans for the future. It is likely that following the new legislation in 1996, these services will be much expanded and become more commonplace.

It is also true that statutory bodies such as the probation service, through its family court welfare arm, have become much more concerned to develop an approach which involves children as much as possible and pays direct attention to their needs. Social services departments, too, may be involved in assessing children's needs and arranging daycare and other support services when children's welfare may be put at risk as a result of parental separation. For example, providing effective and sensitive contact arrangements where children can meet absent parents in neutral and comfortable surroundings is of considerable importance.

A substantial body of skill and experience across the voluntary and statutory sectors has been built up in response to the changing patterns of family life we have observed. However, it is also true to say that the work has largely developed and grown in the absence of any clear consensus of values, or of any lead from sources such as Government which might be felt to have a responsibility to take the initiative. It is to be hoped that the new framework established by the Family Law Act 1996 (see Chapter 5) will markedly improve the situation.

Chapter 3

What happens to children?

What does research tell us?

There now exists a substantial body of research evidence on the effects of family disruption, family conflict and differing family structures, and on the specific effects of separation and divorce. This is helpful in illuminating some of the discussions about the best approaches to family policy, and the proper way to provide services to deal with the consequences of family change. Louie Burghes (*Lone Parenthood and Family Disruption*, 1994), for instance, has carried out an extensive review of the implications for children living in differing family structures, and of family disruption. As she notes, this is a difficult and complex area of research in which to try to draw definitive conclusions, partly because of the problematic issue of singling out possible causes for particular outcomes. It is not always possible to distinguish easily between the effects of 'background' factors, such as social class or family conflict, and specific events, such as any marital breakdown or the occasion of the formal granting of a divorce. Nor is it possible to conduct experiments on families, so it will never be clear what might have happened within a particular family if, say, separation had not taken place. Thus, comparisons between family 'types' are always at best approximate.

Nevertheless, it has proved possible to draw some general conclusions about the implications for children of changing family experiences. For instance, the behaviour of children from disrupted families has been found to be poorer than those from other families, although at the same time it has been suggested that this difference can to a substantial extent be accounted for by the levels of parental conflict before divorce. Children aged between 7 and 16 whose parents divorce are also reported as being likely to be 'unhappy and worried'.

Children from separated and divorced families have been found to achieve lower educational levels than others, notably in maths, although other factors such as social class clearly have an influence, and some of the disparity could be accounted for by lower levels of achievement among children in separated families prior to their parents' parting.

Children from disrupted families have also been found to achieve fewer formal educational qualifications, to acquire lower-status jobs, and to be more at risk of unemployment in adulthood.

Transitions to adulthood, i.e. leaving school, leaving home and starting families, are also likely to occur earlier for children from separated families. In this context, the experience of living in step-families appears to have an additional effect in that this appears to result in young people leaving home earlier than those living in other family structures.

Louie Burghes suggests that there are a number of adverse outcomes for children associated with the separation and divorce of their parents. On the other hand, the association is not always clear-cut, nor does it apply to all families in a given set of circumstances. Children vary by age, gender, experience and ethnic and social origins, and all these factors will have a bearing on their ability to cope with disruption and change.

Counting the cost

It is also apparent that the adverse effects on children whose parents separate may be observed to a degree prior to a 'formal' outcome such as divorce. It is thus difficult to advance the argument that divorce in itself is the sole cause of subsequent difficulties for children.

Nevertheless, even in cases where children experience parental conflict prior to separation, it appears that the parents' decision to part may in turn trigger further negative effects. Lower income is a likely consequence, as is the possibility of less 'availability' of parents for their children, because of their own preoccupations and difficulties and because of physical barriers, such as distance apart. There is thus the possibility of some ambivalence in children's feelings about parental separation. This is apparent even where domestic violence may have occurred within the family.

The outcomes of marital breakdown are thus said to be variable and the effects on children are also likely to vary. This, in turn, makes it difficult to be dogmatic about the proper approach to the problems of marital breakdown to be taken in policy and practice. As Louie Burghes observes, some commentators have tried to explain the effects of disruption on children as part of a process arising from specific family dynamics, rather than as the product of any given structure such as lone parenthood, or the consequence of any specific events such as divorce. It is possible, for instance, to conceive of parental separation happening in quite different circumstances and leading in contrasting ways to divorce over varying timescales. It would be surprising, indeed, to find that divorce itself triggered off the variety and variable intensity of adverse consequences described.

The question of the precise weight to be given to different factors is answered in different ways by other researchers. For instance, the well-known Exeter study (*The Exeter Family Study*, 1996) finds clear evidence of a link between different family types and a range of outcomes for children. The gist of the argument put forward by this study is that children in 're-ordered' families experience more problems than those in 'intact' families, even those where there is parental conflict. By comparing the experiences of 'matched' pairs of children in intact and disrupted families, the Exeter researchers were able to show that children who experienced family break-down also experienced a number of adverse circumstances in their own lives. They were more likely to be 'unhappy'; and they were less likely to have a positive view of themselves. In terms of health, they were reported to be more likely to suffer 'psychosomatic' symptoms such as headaches, stomach aches and nausea. In addition, they were more likely to have had a referral to psychological services.

At school, behavioural problems such as truancy were more evident in children from re-ordered families, and there was some evidence that this group also had more problems with academic work.

At home, children's moods and behaviour were reported to be rather more problematic in a number of respects in families which had undergone change. This might include concerns about negative or hostile moods, or behaviour which parents found disturbing, particularly in step-families.

Children in re-ordered families were also less likely to have contact with grandparents, which they often found upsetting; and family outings and holidays were less frequent, possibly because of lack of money. For children who had experienced family disruption on more than one occasion, these negative consequences appeared to be intensified.

While recognising the effects of continuing conflict, the Exeter researchers point out that most of these adverse effects were stronger for children in families which had broken down than in intact families, even those where conflict levels were reported as high. This has led them to conclude:

parental conflict and financial difficulties are clearly important features of family reorganisation that are associated with adverse outcomes for children. However, in this study it appeared that a more important adverse factor was the loss of a parent and the consequences which included the risk that history would repeat itself with the breakdown of subsequent parental relationships. (p. 60)

Children's responses

Other writers have explored the personal implications of these general observations. Brynna Kroll (*Chasing Rainbows*, 1994), for example, identifies four 'typical' responses by children to parental separation or divorce. She describes children in these categories as 'the parental child', 'the despairing child', 'the retreating child', or 'the angry child'. Her work as a court welfare officer reporting on the needs of children in the context of their parents' divorce has given her a good opportunity to observe the kinds of behaviour displayed by children. Thus, for example, she refers to the protective role taken by some children, often quite young, towards their parents, in a sense taking on aspects of the 'parental' role, when it appears that parents themselves are too distracted to cope with their responsibilities. She describes Sophie, aged 5, who displayed an adult concern for her mother, checking to see if she felt 'alright', caring for her younger brother and in turn offering approval or disapproval of her mother's behaviour. This unfolding situation led to very real confusions about the relative roles and status of Sophie, her mother and younger brother.

According to Brynna Kroll, children in this category were substituting for parents who themselves were struggling to cope, and were thereby losing out on some important aspects of being

27

a child. At the same time, they also found themselves in the position of trying to control a difficult and stressful situation.

The 'despairing child', on the other hand, 'seemed forlorn and lost, sad, tearful, distracted and wistful, and often conveyed a sense of bleakness, yearning or pining'. (p.100) Such children did not respond to stimulation, and seemed unable to play. Livia, for instance, was caught in the middle of an antagonistic custody dispute between her parents, and her confusion and anxiety apparently left her unable to express herself in her meetings with the court welfare officer. She sat still in her chair, reflecting, in Brynna Kroll's view, a real sense of being 'stuck' at the centre of her parents' battles.

Despairing children appeared to be responding to high levels of parental conflict, and the consequent uncertainty and aggression, which were both unsettling and frightening.

The third group, the 'retreating child', is said by Brynna Kroll to revert to an earlier stage of development, probably as a way of drawing attention to his or her own needs, but also in order to return to an earlier stage of greater security. Amjit, for example, wanted to cling on to his memories of his father, who had moved away following his parents' separation. His mother's explicit rejection of his father, whether or not justified, appeared to leave him without an important part of his life. Retreating children typically reverted to behaviour such as thumb-sucking or bed-wetting; this was possibly a means of gaining attention in a frantic situation, but it also represented a need to recover a time of their lives when they felt safe and loved, and life was predictable.

Finally, Brynna Kroll describes the 'angry child', who appeared to be expressing strong feelings primarily as a reflection of the hostility and aggression expressed by parents towards each other. Associated with this, 'angry' children are used as carriers of negative messages between parents and other family members.

Cathy, aged 8, demonstrated her feelings quite graphically in her meetings with the court welfare officer. She is described as 'running round the room pretending to fly a plane' and making a lot of noise which culminated in a chant of 'No, no, no!' She also spoke explicitly about her annoyance with her parents fighting over her. In some ways, such angry reactions may be seen as more healthy than simply 'bottling it all up', but they are also instructive in that they are a direct reflection of parents' own anger and aggressive behaviour towards each other.

These 'types' of reaction from children are, as Brynna Kroll acknowledges, only approximations. As she points out, some children appear to demonstrate more than one type of behaviour, while others may move between categories. In addition, as she rightly observes, there are 'stages' to the divorce experience, and children's reactions are also likely to change, especially as they grow and move through developmental stages.

Long-term effects

The process of change, and the implications of the longer-term effects of divorce, are perhaps best documented by Judy Wallerstein and her colleagues (*Second Chances*, 1989), who have followed a group of divorced families at regular intervals up to 15 years after the event. These studies have shown that children's ages and their stages of development are important in influencing their reaction, but they also indicate that the range of responses is quite similar to that sketched out by Brynna Kroll.

'Sammy Moore', for instance, whose parents divorced when he was seven, exhibited a variety of 'angry' reactions to the event. Apparently he felt a great deal of guilt for what had happened. But as he grew up, he worked through his feelings, with help from counsellors, and with the continued support of both parents. As a young adult, he still appeared to be close to both of them, and this consistency of care had clearly helped him over the years.

In this respect he was perhaps unusual, certainly in the context of the study. For many children adolescence in particular was a difficult and anxious time as their own growth to maturity was overshadowed by continuing concern about their parents and their relationships with them. 'Steve', for instance, was deeply affected by his parents' divorce; then he lost touch with his father, and was never able to come to terms with this. His depression and listlessness persisted into early adulthood. 'Tanya' effectively lost both her parents, with her father never visiting, and her mother working constantly to support the family. In response, it seems, she became involved in a series of short-term sexual relationships from the age of 14. According to Judy Wallerstein and her colleagues Tanya was 'driven' by conflicting emotions of anger at her father, and fear of being alone and unloved. It is not inevitable that young people will suffer long-term damage as a result of their parents' divorce, in their view, but this appears to depend on a number of 'protective' factors, such as positive support from both parents and other relatives.

Despite the powerful evidence of the negative consequences of separation and divorce, a number of other considerations are relevant here. Firstly, conflict and stress are evident in families prior to parental separation. These in themselves, and especially where violence is present, appear to have adverse consequences, as the Exeter study shows. For these children and parents, living under extreme conditions such as the routine experience of violence perpetrated by fathers and other family members, there may be no alternative but to leave. The effects of such experiences are also likely to be long-term and damaging. As a further complication, it is clear that children in such circumstances also appear to retain a high degree of ambivalence about the absent parent.

Equally, for children in stable homes with good quality of care, where living standards are reasonable and parental relationships are good, the effects of the previous separation are less likely to be severe. Judy Wallerstein and her colleagues describe a number of young people who appear to have been able to make the transition to adulthood successfully, and they attribute this to their levels of support and care from parents and others, who manage to surmount their own differences in the interests of their children. 'Rina's' stepfather was the first person in her life who believed in her. His love, care and financial support enabled her to make the transition from delinquent to successful college student. 'Diane's' parents, despite their mutual hostility, worked together to give her the support she needed. Her father retained an active interest and a degree of authority over her after he had left, and he supported her financially through college. Other members of the family, such as her *three* sets of grandparents, also showed consistent care and affection for her. A good quality of family life is not unachievable following the breakdown of parental relationships.

Recognising needs

From these observations, it becomes clear that the relative likelihood of a given outcome as a consequence of parental separation or divorce is unpredictable for any one child or young person. The risks of continuing parental conflict, financial and social insecurity and loss of contact with absent parents or other family members are all well documented, but in various ways these outcomes and their effects can be mitigated. This is not, ultimately, an argument for restricting the availability of divorce, or compelling families to stay together in damaging and dangerous relationships, but for dealing honestly and sensitively with the consequences of parental separation when it occurs.

It is easy to guess generally about the needs of children in relation to their divorcing or divorced parents, but it is better to have a clearer framework against which we can be aware of and better informed about their actual needs.

The domestic context of the impact

Children who do not live with their mother and father can find themselves in a variety of situations. They may be living:

- as a child of a parent bereaved of their spouse and the child's other parent;
- as a child of a single parent with the other parent absent or unknown;
- as a child living with unmarried parents;
- as a child living with a parent whose unmarried partner is not his or her natural parent;
- as a child of a reconstituted family where one of the couple is their step-parent;
- as a child who is being looked after, perhaps as a foster child, away from either parent.

This list is not complete, and is open to further and significant complexity with the addition of a child or children of the substitute parent (e.g. in the case of a reconstituted family). However, change in the substitute parenting circumstances of any of these children will be difficult, threatening and problematic.

While no judgmental or devaluing innuendo is intended against these other family patterns, it has to be said that for a child who has been born and nurtured into a healthy, stable and well-functioning two-parent family, with or without brothers or sisters, this in itself will be a highly positive (if taken-for-granted) experience. However, abrupt circumstantial change in the 'primary group' for such a child could only be one of particular loss and threat.

Of course, where a family has been an inconsistent, chaotic or injurious one, the outcome of parental break-up for the child should be more positive, though not without considerably mixed emotions and anxieties and the reception of a new set of problems, not least about access and the human and detailed domestic implications. Young children are simply not able to conceptualise, and few in the middle of a relationship struggle are able to take anything approaching an objective view.

The nature of the impact

As a general rule, parental matrimonial breakdown and the likelihood of impending divorce will convey the following messages to a child:

- that suddenly everything is in a state of flux;
- that there is no further certainty;
- that they are not the centre of the relationship issue in question (even though they may try and take centre stage in order to attempt to control it);
- that all their relationship patterns may have to be re-learnt;
- that they may end up having to live in a reconstituted family where they may have to fight for a place in a pecking-order among all the siblings;
- that to move away and to lose their home and territorial base will place them at an impossible disadvantage;
- that they are not their parents' priority any more.

A child affected by parental divorce will be inwardly multiply fractured, to varying degrees of severity, according to temperament, resilience potential and the nature of the relationships and circumstances of the particular family. This must be contrasted with children of single parents, for example, who if the parent meets a partner, may be anxious about change and possibly resentful of some inevitable loss and re-ordering of love and attention. But apprehension about change is quite different in kind from being inwardly multiply fractured. Uncertainty about how things will develop is distinct from grief and shock about things falling apart. The child whose parents divorce faces both these challenges, not one.

The 'human spirituality' of a child

The argument may be put in another way in order to demonstrate the point at issue: each of the elements of a child's sense of personhood could be seen to be splitting apart.

These elements of a sense of personhood, or the 'human spirituality' of a child, require support and nurture in five principal areas, and parental divorce invariably causes this process to stall. These elements are:

- The need for the experience of a profound quality of love. This is usually from the child's natural parent(s). Love of this kind gives the child a sense of significance. Being cuddled counts.

- The need for a sense of immediate and ultimate security. This refers both to a sense of 'being safe', and to a feeling of peace with the wider world. This may be dramatised at moments of reassurance during the day, and at the time of being settled down for the night.

- The need for new creative experiences (a) in play and exploration, and also (b) through some personal 'space'

for the experience of inner peace and wonder. The link-
age between these two realms of experience may
sometimes be through the imagination which can
almost instantly be entered or left. For parents or carers
to take a child on visits to new settings has particular
value.

• The need for the affirmation of others. Obviously there
are going to be boundaries, which one has to keep
within in order to enjoy praise and to avoid blame.
Being encouraged for positive behaviour, rather than
admonished for negative, is fundamental to a sense of
usefulness, 'direction' and well-being. (Note the excel-
lent affirmative approach of the Marlborough House
Day Unit, Swindon, and Marlborough NHS Trust.)

• The need for the opportunity of taking part in and
contributing to the social well-being of their family and
neighbourhood, and thus to experience a sense of
community. Being included rather than left out, or left
behind, is very important.

In simplified terms, these five needs reflect the five categories
of 'human spirituality': love, peace, wonder, joy and relatedness.

Impact on a child's 'human spirituality'

Where a child or young person has been looked after by both
natural parents living together in a reasonably effective marriage relationship, these five aspects of 'human spirituality'
should have been developed as a harmonious whole.
However, if there is suddenly a parental divorce, with parents
subsequently living at different places (and even allowing for
suitable access arrangements), then necessarily these five
aspects of nurture will be totally bifurcated. Love will now
come from two different sources and from two different loca-
tions. Security and serenity will be at sea. Sharing new

experiences and having moments of wonder will be jaundiced in the extreme. Encouragement and support will seem hollow. Growth in responsibility and participation will be contrived in that the child or children will have to have a persona in two different situations, and their basic models for responsibility and participation will be seen to have blown up in their faces.

These are strong words and this is frank speaking about the response of the child. But, surely, this is exactly how he or she will feel? This is not to say that it is never right for parents to divorce each other. But it is to say that where parents do choose to divorce each other, the cost to the child or children of the marriage is inevitable, and that all possible means should be taken for that cost to be understood, allowed for and minimised.

Parents who assume that their divorce is not the business of their children, that this is purely the business of the parent and their solicitor, and that the children will not be affected by it, are simply deluding themselves. On the other hand, adults who become overtly over-concerned on the child's or children's behalf could actually raise their existing level of distress.

Basic adjustment needs

Openness rather than secretiveness with children is important; and the imperatives are for building hard on what child–parent trust continues, and for damage limitation.

An immediate outcome of parental divorce for the child is that instead of sharing a home with both parents and of having free and easy access to both of them, meeting them now becomes subject to a timetable and life has a new framework of parental encounter imposed upon it. Everything has to be reconsidered in the light of where the child 'has to be'. Even though the circumstances may cause pressure, the more such a change can be discussed and prepared with the child, the better. In ordinary life, if a parent has to be away for any period, or if a move in accommodation has to take place, this is explained, discussed and prepared over time. Abruptness and suddenness of action make changes more difficult for anyone to handle, not least a child.

Chapter 4

Predicting the effects on children

Responding to change

Significant changes in the way in which we organise our lives are bound to have wider effects. Thus, the well-documented transformation patterns of cohabitation, marriage and divorce will clearly have consequences for those affected, and especially for children who may be singularly powerless to affect what is going on around them.

It is thus important to consider the effects on children after their parent's decision to end their own relationship. For those who respond, whether professionally or personally, to the breakdown of a marriage or a permanent relationship, it is important to understand the likely consequences for children, in order to act sensitively and appropriately.

It is perhaps useful to consider the impact on children under the following headings.

Financial and material

One immediate and clear consequence of parents splitting up is that children's material circumstances will change. Where, as is commonly the case, a wage-earning father leaves the household, immediate reduction in family income will result. Children should benefit by way of maintenance payments, but this is by no means certain and may still represent a shortfall compared to the previous family income.

The children are likely, then, to find themselves worse off as a result of their parents' separation. They may receive less in pocket money, and be less likely to participate in family 'treats' such as outings or holidays.

Domestic circumstances

The breakdown of a marriage may also have a clear and immediate affect on the domestic arrangements with which children may be familiar. They may, for instance, have to move house to a strange neighbourhood or even further afield, with the result that their entire environment has changed; their routines are altered; and they are no longer able to return to safe and familiar places.

Even if the disruption is at a lower level, it is likely that the normal pattern of household life will change, simply because of the need to organise day-to-day activities differently, such as going to school, shopping or attending outside activities. Familiar events may simply no longer take place.

Social change

As a consequence of the changes already outlined, children may well experience social disruption as well. With a move may come a change of school, and the loss of valued friendships. Even without a move, there may be less time and opportunity to meet up with friends. It may be more difficult to afford to keep up with friends who, in turn, might demonstrate a change of attitude. The child's own understandable preoccupation with what is going on in the family may additionally make her or him less fun to be with, and friends may respond accordingly.

Family relationships

Not only will parents' separation have an obvious effect on family relationships, but it will probably have more subtle consequences too. Firstly, it is almost certain that one parent, at least, will not be around when the child needs him or her. The other parent may also be less available because of having to take on extra domestic tasks, and possibly extra paid work, in order to improve the family income.

In addition, other family members will be affected. Brothers and sisters of course will be directly involved, and it is possible that internal family tensions will increase. Other relatives, too, such as cousins, aunts and uncles, and particularly grandparents, will also be affected. In some cases this may mean virtual or total loss of contact with a loved relative. In other cases it may mean having to listen and respond to 'tales' about one or other parent. The extended family has the most scope for rumours and allegations to develop, which, regardless of their accuracy, can have a negative effect on children who are made aware of them.

Personal factors

The loss to the child represented by parental separation may also be direct and personal, arising from reduced contact with (definitely) one or (probably) both parents. This may result in a reduction in what is known as 'quality time' – i.e. time for personal talks and confidences or favourite activities with one parent in particular. There may be a reduction in 'availability' – just a knowledge that someone is there when needed; and there is no longer a choice of which parent to go to for help over particular matters. A significant example of this would be the opportunity to discuss the onset of menstruation, or developing sexual feelings, with the parent that the young person feels most comfortable with.

Psychological consequences

In one sense, the psychological consequences of parental separation are likely to interact with and perhaps reinforce the effects of the other problems already outlined. A very wide range of psychological effects may arise from the child's experience of their parents splitting up, including, for example, guilt, where the young person feels somehow responsible for their parents' separation, whether by imposing an unfair burden on their relationship, or by virtue of something specific said or done.

The child or young person may feel anger at one or both parents. The absent parent may be blamed for desertion or indifference to the child, and in addition he or she is unavailable to allow the child to vent his or her angry feelings. There may also be unresolved feelings of anger at the behaviour of the absent parent prior to leaving. The remaining parent may be blamed for failing to prevent the breakdown, for failing to offer adequate protection to the child, or simply for being unable to provide the range of 'services' offered by the other parent.

It is likely that the child will feel insecure and uncertain, partly because of so many changes in lifestyle and family circumstances. This is in many ways a perfectly natural reaction to significant change such as transferring from one school to another or moving house. It is, however, compounded where one of the key insulating factors against insecurity (i.e. one parent) is actually seen as one of its causes.

Insecurity, in turn, is likely to have an effect on self-confidence and ability to withstand 'knocks'. This may be evident in declining school performance, less care about appearance, and perhaps a less open and cheerful demeanour.

Other psychological stresses are likely to be evident. The child may experience a sense of loss and betrayal akin to the impact of bereavement. There may be increased pressure on the child or young person who now feels the need to take on adult responsibilities to replace the lost parent. There may be a sense of powerlessness and inadequacy induced by the feeling of being unable to influence or change what is going on, despite what might be quite explicit pleas to one or both parents to change their minds. There may be a feeling of worthlessness and rejection, almost abandonment by the parent who leaves home. This, of course, may have a differential effect depending on the genders of parent and child, where, say, a mother's apparent rejection of a daughter may have powerful connotations.

More mundane feelings such as loneliness and isolation are also likely to be experienced by children in these circumstances. The loss of a close confidant may remove the only opportunity to share strong feelings and to ask urgent questions. Many more of the child's concerns may simply be 'bottled up'.

A change for the better?

Of course, it must be acknowledged that this catalogue of potentially adverse consequences of parental separation or marriage breakdown can be offset by the sense of relief of bringing to an end a particularly difficult or stressful situation. Thus, for children suffering violence or sexual abuse, or those simply enduring constant friction between parents, there may be clear gains from an eventual separation. In addition, it is possible that they may find themselves better off because money is being shared between family members rather than held back by one parent. There may indeed be a sense of overall freedom resulting from the departure of one oppressive family member. We must acknowledge that not all marriages are perfect.

Ages and stages

Not only do children's reactions to divorce vary, but they are also likely to change depending on their age and the length of time that has passed since their parents separated. Some authors (e.g. Ayalon and Flasher, 1993) have categorised children's reactions. According to them, there are three stages at which different kinds of reaction are to be found in children.

Early childhood

Young children are likely to display distress or concern openly, and to demonstrate very clear signs of regression. Thus, crying and emotional distress may become more common, and in some cases sleeping problems and bed-wetting may reflect an increase in worrying and uncertainty. They are likely to become less adventurous, more clinging, and passive. Among boys, researchers have observed greater signs of aggression, while girls may become more introverted.

The middle years

While older children may become less extreme in their reactions to divorce, and may demonstrate their feelings in other ways, the apparent evidence of increased ability to cope should not be allowed to disguise the fact that they are likely still to have strong feelings about their parents' separation or divorce. Some of these children will appear to adopt a very mature approach. However, this is likely to be a mask for feelings of insecurity or even anger. Brynna Kroll (*Chasing Rainbows*, 1994) describes the case of 'Camilla', who appeared detached and described her parents as if they were 'wayward children'. However, beneath this serene surface she had strong feelings of anger towards both parents, who appeared to be using her for their own ends.

Adolescence

While adolescents are perhaps better equipped than younger children to bring a longer-term perspective to bear on the situation, it is by no means certain that they will easily resolve the difficulties and stresses caused by their parents' divorce or separation, even when that has taken place many years previously. Thus, adolescents may be seen to be realistic about what has happened, and better able to express their feelings directly and with a degree of maturity. However, their own experiences are likely to leave them with a reservoir of fear

43

about both their own personal security, and about their own ability to form secure and stable relationships. In addition, there is evidence of continuing difficulty in other areas of their lives, such as school, where continuing uncertainty and lingering depression may reduce their performance and their level of achievement.

The pressure to find security and certainty in their own lives may push young people towards early, perhaps over-optimistic and oppressive commitments to partners, with the result that they may form relationships, marry and have children earlier than other young people, in ways that are likely to leave these relationships in turn at risk of disruption and breakdown.

It seems, therefore, that there are differences in the reactions of children and young people to divorce, depending on the period of childhood or adolescence which they have reached. In addition, it seems to be the case that, as with bereavement, reactions will change and modify over time. Thus, early reactions are likely to be 'raw', particularly for young children with powerful expressions of distress, anger and sorrow. These are clearly upsetting, and there may be a wish on the part of concerned adults to minimise these displays of strong feeling. On the other hand, there are also clear risks in denying the opportunity to say exactly what they think, and to express themselves forcefully.

At subsequent stages, children and young people will show a greater readiness to adapt to the changed circumstances of their parents, almost irrespective of their age at the time. They may become quite well-versed in developing coping strategies and, indeed, in providing support and resources for their own parents. This ability to cope, however, itself places heavy demands on children and young people, and it may create longer-term difficulties, particularly if it has a negative impact on their own prospects, for example in schooling.

There appears to be a further stage, at least judging by the work of Wallerstein and Blakeslee (*Second Chances*, 1989). Children and young people appear to carry with them longer-term feelings of insecurity; they appear to be uncertain about their ability to form mature adult relationships in their own right; and, in some cases, unresolved feelings appear to be linked with continuing feelings of depression and underachievement.

Being prepared

It is evident, therefore, that the effects of separation and divorce are many and, in some cases, long-standing. There is a need to recognise this and to be prepared to provide support and encouragement to mitigate these damaging consequences. Subsequent chapters will consider the challenges faced by all those concerned with the long-term welfare of the children affected.

It is important to recognise that many of the adverse consequences depicted can be avoided, by parents working co-operatively even though separated, and by ensuring that close attention is paid to children, and that their needs are responded to effectively. In this way, the need for reassurance and for underpinning self-confidence can be met.

There should be no sense of inevitability about the kind of negative outcomes described, because of the human capacity to build in safeguards and to provide positive support, once the risks and dangers of separation are acknowledged. The research evidence available confirms these observations, suggesting that other members of the community, opinion formers and religious and secular bodies should not pass judgement or compound feelings of inadequacy, but should take a forward-looking view of the need to protect children, and promote their welfare and their interests into the future.

PART TWO

Dealing with the consequences

Chapter 5

Meeting our responsibilities: the legal and practical context

The new law: the Family Law Act 1996

The Family Law Act 1996 represents the culmination of a debate about the nature of marriage and family life, and the responsibilities of adults to each other and to their children. The Act attempts to achieve two things, which might at first glance appear contradictory. It provides the basis for the recognition of the value of marriage and stable relationships; and at the same time it recognises the need to prepare effectively to deal with the consequences when marital relationships break down.

It is not enough simply to stress the value and the strength of marriage in a context where a significant proportion of marriages, and indeed other parental relationships such as cohabitations, come to an end. Dealing with the consequences of such events is a responsibility for which provision must be made. Nor is it possible to legislate to prevent marital break-down. Once this is recognised, the need for sound policy and good practice dictates that proper and effective mechanisms are put in place to deal with the difficulties that inevitably arise from the failure of relationships involving children. It is in this spirit that the 1996 Act has been passed by parliament with a substantial degree of all-party support.

What the Act says

The central change heralded by the 1996 Act, and the one which has caused most controversy, alters the basis by which marital breakdowns are ratified. Although, in fact, the 1969 Divorce Law Reform Act claimed to do away with 'fault' as the ground for divorce, it merely shifted the concept back a stage, ensuring that it retained a significant part as one of the 'proofs' of irretrievable breakdown. Thus, 'proof' of adultery or unreasonable behaviour remained significant routes towards providing sufficient evidence to enable courts to ratify the end of a marriage. Not only did this necessarily introduce a sour and adversarial note into proceedings, but it also had a distorting effect. This was because these routes provided the quickest way to secure a divorce, usually in a matter of months, rather than having to wait two years for divorce based on the more neutral reason of 'separation'. Thus, a demonstration of unfaithfulness or mistreatment (often quite spurious, it must be said) provided a shortcut to the desired outcome, thereby introducing elements both of acrimony and of farce into proceedings.

Retention of the concept of 'fault' therefore neither discouraged divorce, nor did it deter those who would be held in law to be culpable from making use of the options available if it meant a quicker end to the marriage. A change was clearly necessary, although some MPs and others, including bishops, were concerned at this development, fearing that divorce would become more acceptable and thus easier to secure.

The Family Law Act attempts to simplify proceedings in the event of marital breakdown, to remove the elements of conflict and dishonesty arising from fault-based procedures, and also, effectively, to lengthen the average period couples must wait for divorces to be ratified. Since they must now wait for a period of at least a year, this will more than double the average waiting time for a divorce prior to the new legislation.

Following initial notification that the marriage has broken down, a period of at least a year (18 months where children are involved) must elapse before the divorce is granted. This, in the view of the government, and indeed most commentators, is a sufficient period to assess whether the breakdown is irrevocable, to provide an opportunity to think again, to consider the consequences including the effects on children, and to resolve outstanding questions about the allocation of property and children's future welfare.

Safeguards for children

The new legislation provides a number of safeguards to ensure that separating couples have every opportunity to consider fully the implications of their decision, and to plan properly for their children. At all stages in this process, the interests of children are recognised and this Act makes it clear that their needs are paramount in the same spirit as the Children Act. Full information about the processes surrounding separation and divorce available is to be provided, which should be age appropriate; and it is to be hoped that advice and counselling services will be expanded to meet the new needs. In addition, it is planned to offer mediation in all cases of marital breakdown in order to enable couples to come together to consider their options, and to make joint plans for the future. It has been repeatedly stressed, and the Act underlines this, that the welfare and development of children must be a paramount consideration, and it is felt that mediation has an important contribution to make in putting children first.

In the event of mediation failing, or if it is inappropriate, say, for reasons of abuse or domestic violence, safeguards are provided in that the adjudicating court must be satisfied regarding the children's future welfare, and the option is available to the court to require additional assessments of their long-term needs. These assessments will be carried out by qualified and experienced child-welfare professionals. Based on such assessments, the court may then make additional orders aimed at providing for the long-term security of the children concerned.

At every stage it is intended that children will be offered the opportunity to express their own views and wishes in ways suited to their age and understanding. They will not, however, be burdened with the responsibility of 'choosing' between their parents.

Mediation

Mediation is intended to be central to the newly established processes for securing a satisfactory outcome for those affected by divorce, and for children in particular. Advice, which is not compulsory, can be offered at various stages of proceedings, by courts and by others providing information and services, recommending couples to make use of it, if it is seen as appropriate.

Mediation is now well established, both in the UK and in other parts of the world, such as Australia and New Zealand, as an effective means of achieving understanding and broad agreement between separating couples about a range of domestic and financial issues, and particularly about the care and upbringing of their children. In the UK a number of voluntary bodies have invested considerable effort into developing mediation services, drawing up practice standards, and establishing a sound basis for training and accreditation of those involved. A number of reports and studies have been completed which demonstrate its value, although it is recognised that there are limitations to what it can achieve.

Typically, mediation will involve a series of meetings between the separating couple, at which their differences are aired and attempts made to resolve them under the guidance of one (or two) trained and qualified professional(s). The aim of this process is to achieve a full airing of the facts and feelings which act as impediments to co-operative decision-making; to attempt to resolve the disagreements which these represent; and to find a sound basis on which future plans can be made. Once this is achieved, potentially contentious questions may be resolved amicably, such as the issue of where the children will live, and for how long, under what conditions they will have contact with one or other parent, ground rules for family discipline, which school the children will attend, and their religious and cultural upbringing.

Continuing concerns

Mediators do not claim to be able to resolve every intractable problem. It has been suggested that because settlements based on mediation are essentially voluntary and unenforceable, this may be to disadvantage weaker participants, particularly women, as well as children who may not have a direct say in the process.

In addition, there are some consequences of a relationship breakdown over which mediators can have little control. The rigid formula applied by the Child Support Act, for example, may introduce additional tensions and disagreements into discussions between parents, which are difficult to resolve. The best that can be achieved in this situation is perhaps a willingness to abide by the rules as laid out, and to understand the other participant's position, since the apportionment of financial responsibility for children is likely to be legally non-negotiable in many cases.

Additionally, various safeguards have been built into the practice of mediation itself, so that, for instance, two mediators are often used in order to avoid unconscious bias, or the unintentional application of pressure to arrive at a solution without considering all the implications. Clearly it is also important to be able to direct participants to other sources of informed advice on matters such as legal representation, taxation, housing advice, or the Child Support Agency, which are likely to go beyond the mediators' sphere of expertise.

However practice develops, mediators in some instances are able to draw on legal and financial expertise in order to aid deliberations. In addition, there have been a number of interesting developments aimed at securing the participation (either directly or indirectly) of children in the mediation context. Above and beyond this, however, concerns remain about the adequacy of the safeguards provided. It is clear that the view of mediators as a 'cheap option' may result in undue pressure to seek solutions by these means even where this is clearly inappropriate. It will remain important that, where children are at risk, where their welfare cannot be safeguarded, or simply where mediated agreements are unrealistic, there must be recourse to more formal powers such as those held by the courts and the statutory agencies to protect children and to promote their interests. Importantly, the Family Law Act itself does not build in incentives which might favour mediation over the pursuit of court action. When legal proceedings are pursued, the provision for courts to enquire into children's welfare in ratifying divorce settlements is intended to involve rather more than a cursory glance over written agreements should there be any cause for doubt about the suitability or achievability of the arrangements proposed.

Looking to the future

Clearly, the effectiveness of the new legal framework for divorce will only be tested fully as practice develops, but it is important that it remains under close scrutiny, in the context of a major shift in the way in which marriage breakdown is dealt with in this country. We are entering uncharted territory.

With the incorporation of mediation as a central element in procedures for dealing with family breakdown, there will additionally be a need to develop effective professional practice and appropriate standards in training and accreditation of staff, as well as the kind of legal safeguards already discussed. In addition, these new provisions will see the emergence of a strong professional discipline, and associated organisational frameworks. Thus, for all those working with, or advising families on the subject of separation or divorce and dealing with the consequences, there will be a need to be informed about how this much-changed service will operate, and how its services will be made available.

It is likely that mediation services will be provided under the auspices of the National Family Mediators Association, the body to which most existing services and practitioners belong, and which has been responsible for developing practice standards, accreditation schemes and training resources. However, it appears that individual services will operate independently within this overall framework, funded partly by grants and partly by case fees. Mediators are likely to be drawn from a range of social work, psychology and legal backgrounds; and services may be provided privately through the voluntary sector or partly by statutory bodies such as the probation service. It thus appears that service availability may be variable depending on the level of resources available locally, and whether or not mediation services have been readily available in the past. This kind of factor would also affect the ease with which services can be approached by those seeking help or advice.

Further complexity is likely to arise with the roles of Relate (whose primary function is marriage counselling) and the probation service (which has traditionally provided court reports in divorce cases). Both of these agencies appear to have a role in enabling couples to resolve difficulties, but they tend to operate at rather different points in the process than do mediators – Relate will usually become involved before the decision to separate and the probation service after a case has been referred to the court for adjudication.

It is important that those concerned with advising parents about separation and its consequences do understand the distinctions, and the fact that they are sometimes blurred, in order to try and ensure that approaches are made to the appropriate agency, where these are felt to be necessary. Nevertheless, the emergence of a strong new discipline in the form of mediation, and the emphasis emerging from the new legislation and elsewhere, on problem-solving, rather than heated confrontations, is an important change of tone in the context of divorce and separation.

Despite the complexities and uncertainties, this significant change in philosophy is to be welcomed. The new legal framework is explicit in highlighting needs and rights of children experiencing their parents' separation or divorce. It builds in safeguards to ensure that these needs are addressed, and it provides effective mechanisms by which the adults concerned can come to an informed decision about the future of their children.

Chapter 6

The challenge to the Church

Of corporate penitence

The normal life cycle of a marriage passes through courtship and then the early, middle and later years. Good marriages – especially as they progress through the different stages – simply do not exist without effort. If marriage is acknowledged as requiring careful thought, attention and 'maintenance' from each partner in order to create an ongoing, loving and workable relationship of quality, the Church must realise that a couple will benefit from the caring and imaginative friendship and support of their community of faith in order to effect this.

A failed marriage of Church members is therefore to some extent the failure of the Church community also.

Of addressing corporate positive support

The particular challenges to the Church raised by divorce include:

- How can the ministry of the Church promote conciliation or mediation without prejudice to the possibility of reconciliation?

- How can a child or children of the marriage be helped to live in the future with divided loyalties and possibly with a brother or sister who may feel or see things differently?

- How can the separating partners be assisted to end their marriage without rubbishing or erasing the positives of that relationship?

- How can the Church community adjust, and even give a lead, to ministering and relating to the separating partners as single persons again (and to the children as children of divorcees) rather than resorting to denial?

- How can the separating partners be helped to end their marital relationship and begin a new and co-operative co-parental relationship?

- How can the Church community look for a high level of commitment from those seeking to be married (or re-married) and at the same time provide good standards of care for those suffering marital breakdown without inconsistency?

- How can the Church help the partners of a broken marriage and their children to emerge from the experience with hope?

Of developing a personal strategy

In the light of these challenges, a local Church should discuss and establish a pastoral strategy towards those whose marriages have failed, such as the following:

1   To offer a gentle and friendly commendation of the merits of mediation and, where appropriate, sensitively to remind about the option of reconciliation.

2   To hold in mind that adults but especially children and young people suffering a loss of security and stability need the assurance of continuing friendships and acceptance as anchor points.

3   To be ready to re-learn and respect (and to begin to help any children to re-learn and respect) the former husband and wife as individuals dissociated from their former relationship (neither highlighting nor erasing any good memories and aspects of that relationship).

4   To be willing to assist in the healing process which the divorce will inevitably require for children and adults (probably through the showing of simple tender, loving care) – rather than thoughtlessly to exacerbate the hurt of the breakdown.

5   To seek the renewal of Almighty God in the sense of loss and guilt where a marriage has failed to survive, and where children are torn and troubled, and to be ready to offer a liturgical expression marking the end of a relationship (and/or of one stage of parenting) and the opportunity of a new start.

6   To review congregational supportiveness to others in their marriages and to facilitate natural and balanced marital enrichment and parenting support so far as reasonably possible.

7   To facilitate a temporary reversal of the process of good neighbourliness, so that those suffering marital break-down (or parental divorce) who do not have the energy to have time for others, receive consideration from others in return.

Of providing liturgical recognition

So far as liturgy is concerned, it is worth knowing that there are two very worthwhile forms of service marking the end of a marriage which the separating partners might ask to be used with them: either singly, or perhaps even as a couple (though this might be relatively rare). The first is to be found in *Liturgy and Learning through the Life Cycle*, by John H. Westerhoff III (a priest of the Episcopal Church of the USA) and William H. Willimon. In Chapter 8 'A Service for a Recognition of a Divorce' is given. Consideration of the children of the former marriage is very specific:

(i)   the Confession of the Divorced Individual(s) includes the phrase 'I have sinned especially against .... and our child(ren)';

(ii) the Declarations include a response to the question 'Will you share responsibility with .... for the welfare of your child(ren), realizing that the parent–child relationship is not broken?'; and

(iii) the prayers include the petition 'For their child(ren) and that he/she (they) may continue to know the love of their parents and above all know the love of a heavenly Father. May she/he (they) share in your newness.'

The second, 'At the Ending of a Marriage', is contained in *Occasional Celebrations of the Anglican Church of Canada*. This service is based in part on 'A Service for the Ending of a Marriage' in Anne Tanner's *Treasures of Darkness*. Reference to children is made in the Intercessions 'for all whose lives have been affected by this ending of a marriage'. The prayer for them is as follows:

> God of wisdom and understanding
> whose blessed Son Jesus loved children
> and blessed them,
> bless the children of N. and N.
> Strengthen them, calm their fears,
> heal their wounds.
> Help them to grow in the knowledge of your love.
> Comfort them,
> that they may know the newness of life
> that can come from sadness and brokenness.
> Keep them in your loving care, today and always.

The prayer 'for family and friends who are divided' is also very appropriate and helpful and includes reference to grandparents, whose role in family breakdown (especially if not interfering and so far as possible non-judgemental) can be of great significance in providing an experience of continuity for a child.

It has to be said that few persons in Britain would appear to opt for a public or private service of this sort. Most would not know that some tested models were available from other parts of the Anglican Communion, though no such service is approved by the Church of England or the Church in Wales. Awareness of pastoral practice in this respect from other parts of the Anglican Communion would be important when evaluating the *ad hoc* creative responses of certain parochial clergy, as has been reported, for example, in Great Yarmouth, Norwich and Great Horton, Bradford.

It is suggested that this is best undertaken slowly and thoughtfully, with a person of distinct religious commitment and arising out of a relationship of pastoral counselling, with the individual participating over a period in the actual building and drawing-up of the service so that it expresses exactly the feelings, concerns and circumstances of the individual concerned. Those present should be people with whom the individual is comfortable, and who themselves would wish to attend. Some notion of 'automatic and standard provision' (as opposed to guidelines and outline suggestions as resource) would not seem either fitting or sensitive. The presence of a child or children at such a service would need consideration from their point of view, but as a general principle would seem potentially helpful for them.

In the event of re-marriage, and a Service of Blessing and Dedication after a Civil Marriage being held, the preparation should afford a pastoral opportunity for meeting any children, and the following prayer is suggested for inclusion in the Service:

For the child or children of the couple

> O God our heavenly Father, we pray for
> ....
> that his/her/their needs may be acknowledged
> and his/her/their individuality nurtured.
> Grant that the love between N. and N. may in a
> special way bring him/her/them happiness and
> security.
> Bless this new family, that in sharing
> their life with one another, this child/each of
> these children may find personal encouragement
> and enrichment in his/her/their pilgrimage of
> faith amidst the adventure of life.
> Grant this through Jesus Christ our Lord. Amen.

Of a constructive approach to the legal process

Although we might well wish it otherwise, the law has an effect on people's ideas and standards, although it should only set a framework which enables orderly problem resolution.

The response of the Board for Social Responsibility of the Church of England General Synod to the Lord Chancellor's consultation paper, in preparation for the new Family Law Act, was both thorough and constructive, though not over-extended in its somewhat compressed consideration of children. The following extracts are, however, pertinent:

> 3.12. In seeking to meet the objectives of the law
> governing dissolution of marriages ... it is impor-
> tant to bear in mind the consequences of divorce
> for the children as well as the couple. Children
> suffer trauma when their parents are in conflict.

The trauma can be reduced if the conflict between the parents can be reduced. Children will generally benefit from maintaining a good relationship with both their parents even if they are not living together after separation or divorce. The divorce system should not jeopardise the chances of their doing so.

3.13   Couples also experience a good deal of stress as a result of marriage breakdown and the divorce process. Reducing the conflict between the couple would offer a more positive atmosphere in which they could reflect on whether their marriage was really over and, if so, come to terms with the fact that they need to make new living arrangements for themselves and their children. The reduction of conflict may also help both parties to acknowledge their responsibility for what went wrong with the marriage.

It is important for the success of re-marriage that there is some understanding of what has gone wrong in the past. (*Divorce Law Reform: The Government's Proposals*, 1994)

The criteria of the Church towards a constructive divorce process might be said to be as follows:

1   A process which provides seriously for the option of reconciliation.

2   A process which maximises practical consideration for the welfare of children.

3   A process which encourages the development of a stance of mutual respect between the parties – and for their religious faith or value system.

4   A process which contributes to the maintenance of personal dignity and the exercise of balanced judgement on the part of both parties by requiring high

professional standards on the part of those who work with them.

5   A process which discourages any form of exploitation or intimidation and which thereby limits the risk of further damage.

6   A process which requires such considerations as possession of the matrimonial home, a framework of arrangements for the ongoing parenting of the children and decisions about finance to be arrived at prior to the legal moment of divorce and not to be postponed endlessly thereafter.

7   A process which acknowledges the need for and place of good pastoral counselling for both parties and for their children, and which thereby promotes the building-up of positive post-marital functioning and goodwill.

Of being a child-orientated Church

A parishioner leaving a Church service remarks, meaning well, to the vicar, 'Thank you for a lovely and quiet service, vicar . . . it was so nice without the children.' It is remarkable how adult-orientated rather than child-orientated a Church can be.

In The Methodist Church Division of Social Responsibility report *Preparing for Christian Marriage* (1996, section 5.8) the Church's support to marriage and family life at all stages of the life cycle is demonstrated as:

●   An annual service for the re-affirmation of marriage vows

●   Regular prayers in the Church's intercessions for marriages, families and single people

●   Access for couples to courses for marriage enrichment and to skilled counsellors for marriages in difficulties

- Encouragement to church members to train as marital counsellors or as family mediators
- Parenting programmes

This is all to be commended. And perhaps it is just too much to expect marriage preparation to move beyond where people actually are and the dynamics of their current state of relationship. Pointers may of course be given for help in the future.

But how about complementary support for children and young people growing up, especially inclusive of those affected by the divorce of their parents and the tensions of becoming a member of a reconstituted family? Could not corresponding provision be made by the Church for children and young people – including those affected by parental divorce and living in a broken family or a step-family situation:

- to have a place in any Service for the Renewal of Marriage Vows (e.g. 'Renewal of Marriage Vows or On the Anniversary of a Marriage' in *Occasional Services of the Church of Canada*) in which their parents participate?
- to be included, and to have the opportunity of having their special petitions included, in the Church's intercessions?
- to have the opportunity to join in courses on family life enrichment?
- to have access to skilled counsellors with experience in working with those with parent difficulties?
- to have the opportunity of experiencing Childhood and Youth programmes which face up to family breakdown?
- We need to remember the special needs of the child in Church life.

Chapter 7

The challenge to the individual Church member

In this chapter we seek to answer the question, 'What can I do to help?' Ten suggestions are given below; many are to do with attitude formation, since not every child or young person who is affected by the divorce of their parents will wish to talk about it, however much they may need to. Nevertheless, they can be helped if adults with whom they have contact are generally aware of their pressures and are thoughtful in the light of where they will be 'coming from' as regards the worship and activities of the Church.

It should also be said that these suggestions must be set in the wider context of children and young people with other challenges, difficulties and problems with which a Church congregation should also be seeking to be contructively helpful. The effect of divorce on a child is akin to an inward multiple fracture, of varying degrees of severity, arising from a division in the primary source of love, security, new and creative experiences, praise and social involvement. A congregation can be a therapeutic community which understands this but at the same time realises that with proper care, support and time, fractures, even multiple fractures, can heal (although they may carry some degree of inherent weakness in the face of excessive strain). The essential attitude for the congregation to adopt is one which does not hark back, but which seeks to reinforce a child's natural potential for resilience.

1   Affirming resilience

The studies on factors of child resilience by Stefan Vanistendael of the International Catholic Child Bureau, Geneva, are much to be commended. In speaking about some building bricks for resilience, Vanistendael itemises:

- having social networks and unconditional acceptance;
- having the capacity to discover some order, sense and meaning in life;
- having a variety of skills;
- having self-esteem;
- having the gift of humour.

2   Empowering godparents

On being invited to become the godfather to a friend's child in 1945, Robert Graves said:

> I think the godfather's job in this modern world is always to be the chap to whom the godchild writes if he or she has got into a real jam and needs to be bailed out, or fished out of a stew; and with whom he/she goes to stay, uninvited, at times of emotional crisis. (*Broken Images: Selected Letters of Robert Graves, 1914–1946*, Hutchinson, 1982)

There is no doubt that from the point of view of the Church, godparents are significant in caring for the interests of a child who has been baptised and whose parents are divorcing or who have been divorced. The choice of godparents must have been agreed by both parents at the time of baptism and their names are entered in the publicly available Baptismal Register at the parish church concerned.

The duties of godparents may be summarised as follows:

To represent the Church

- through embodying the welcome of the Body of Christ;
- through being a 'bridge of belonging' between Church and child;
- through sincerity, thankfulness, thoughtfulness and fun.

To support the parents

- through lasting friendship;
- through affirming good patterns of parenting;
- through endorsing their links with the household of God.

To encourage their godchild

- through play, story-telling, games, activities and talk;
- through private prayer (especially at baptismal anniversary);
- through ongoing contact, dependability and availability.

Godparents may find the opening sections of *Children and Holy Communion* by Diana Murrie and Steve Pearce to be of interest, especially pages 5, 13 and 14.

It will be immediately recognised that where parental divorce occurs, the support of the parents by the godparents will be bifurcated; double the effort will be required to support two separated parents.

Encouragement of the godchild by the godparents in the event of parental divorce will need to take on a much higher priority, and godparents should be encouraged to be proactive in this respect rather than retiring and self-shielding from possible difficulty.

The report of a Working Party of the Board for Social Responsibility, *Something to Celebrate: Valuing Families in Church and Society* contains this practical advice in Chapter 8 which could be taken as a simple five-point guide for godparents:

It will greatly assist the family if they can be helped to:

- tell their children a coherent story of what has happened and why;
- maintain relationships with both 'sides' of the wider family;
- grieve for what is lost and cannot be restored;
- hold on to and treasure what was good and of value in their past relationship;
- approach the future realistically in terms of the inevitable changes in life style, social life and financial provision.

3   Upholding access as a right of the child

Congregations and especially Clergy, Sunday School and Youth Leaders and Directors of Music need to note that the issue of 'access' is best seen as the right of the child to access to both his or her parents, rather than the right of the parents of access to the child. Doubtless with the best of intentions, groups of one sex or another campaigning for a father or mother's right of access to their child (and for an increased amount of it) frequently miss the all-important point that the paramount right we are talking about is the right of the child to have access to them, rather than the other way round.

Access is an issue which causes heartache and tension in many cases, not least when arrangements are changed or agreements and understandings eroded or broken.

Access patterns need to be worked out to suit the child or children concerned in the light of the particular parental circumstances. Perhaps no hard and fast rules are possible. However, it is worth saying that church congregations and organisations should try and support children of divorcing or divorced parents by minimising disruption on the one hand and unpredicatability on the other.

4 Reminding others of the awkwardnesses of access

As an example of disruption, some children find the continuous short-term breaks with the other parent very difficult to handle. For such children a more extended period during each school holiday may be easier to cope with than every weekend.

As an example of unpredictability, the family with several children where one parent has moved to another house some ten minutes away might be able to cope with the arrangements of living alternate nights and alternate weekends at the different houses, and having, therefore, two bedrooms and two wardobes each, but what they may not be able to cope with easily is if this system is altered so that they find themselves suddenly staying with one parent for two nights running instead of the single night as usual.

Allowance has to be made for the fact that children going away for an access visit will have a period of expectation and anticipation (positive, negative or mixed) and on return will go through a period of reaction and readjustment (positive, negative or mixed). Bearing in mind that both parents will also be going through some inner emotions of anticipation and readjustment, and that there is likely to be some subliminal 'chemistry' between them and their child or children, a highly sensitive and delicate scenario will begin to be seen. If one adds to this the anticipations and reactions of children of other partners with whom the child may have to live and socialise and establish themselves in some sort of pecking order, which will be much easier for some than for others, it will be understood that the children who manage this pattern of life successfully and with good humour are incredibly resilient and deserve considerable credit for their life skills.

5   Enabling access in cases of difficulty

Of the practical care offered by Churches, the 'front room availability' scheme organised by the Mothers' Union for children meeting with their parents on access visits is a very positive one.

6   Encouraging 'inclusiveness' in prayers and at festivals

Sadly, the great Christian festivals such as Christmas, intended as times of peace and goodwill, can be occasions for considerable conflict and even the seeking of court injunctions over who stays with whom and for how long.

With those living with one parent and having access to the other, Mothering Sunday needs to be balanced by the observance of Father's Day. However, church observances on these occasions need to incorporate an intimation of empathy for those whose parents are living apart and are no longer married. Children must be free to respect and grow in affection for their step-parent, but at the same time be free to give primary respect and love to their natural parents: and this needs to be borne in mind when family festivals are organised by the faith community.

7   Suggesting devotional pathways

On the spiritual side, children and young people may sometimes enquire how they should pray for their parents, and in particular, 'should I pray for them to be come together again?' This is a hard question to answer, but there are two key points. The first is that God wants us to tell him what we really want and how we really feel, because he is our Heavenly Father, so it can never be wrong to ask. The second is that while it may not be realistic to pray for parental reconciliation, we can always pray for separating parents to be not lovers nor haters of each other but co-operative colleagues or friends.

It may not be easy for a child or young person whose parents are divorcing or who are divorced to speak of, let alone openly pray for, the 'other' parent. A private prayer for such a child or young person is included in the Prayers at the conclusion of this book, as is a prayer for use by a child or young person if lighting a candle for both their parents in a church or cathedral.

St Christopher (July 27), the carrier of children across deep and maybe troubled waters, and St Anne, the Mother of the Blessed Virgin Mary (July 26), are saints whose attributes may give comfort to a child or young person with parental tensions.

8 Making literature available to children and young people

It is important that the church bookstall, the Children's Church leaflet table or the Youth Club information rack should include some literature which may be of help to those suffering parental divorce. A short resource list is included in an Appendix to this book.

9 Including mediation in church study programmes

Church members, especially those with insight into and experience of the principles and good practice of mediation, should seek to have this subject included, where appropriate, in Church study programmes, not least so that Church members can play a positive part in supporting couples during the greatly extended period to be allowed for mediation under the provisions of the Family Law Act 1996, probably with effect from around 1998.

10 Encouraging clear and careful parental thinking

The decision to divorce is obviously a personal one, and, except in extreme cases, invariably difficult. While some people may be able to arrive at the decision relatively simply, and never look back, others may retain a degree of ambivalence for many years.

Perhaps a straightforward rule of thumb might be to think along the lines that divorce is an appropriate path once a marital relationship has passed from being a positive and life-enhancing experience, to becoming a negative relationship to the point of being irretrievably damaging, destructive and deleterious.

For the Christian, the dilemma lies in distinguishing between the duty of being willing to go the second mile, and the discernment of knowing when it is appropriate to shake off the dust of one's shoes against a quite unreasonably and impossibly hardened situation. This decision has to be left to individual conscience, although a pastoral counsellor may well be exercised in the case of someone who appears too entrapped to be able to use their freedom of choice in the interests of their own basic welfare, and of that of their children.

Christian marriage is a covenant, and both parties undertake to love, comfort, honour, protect and remain faithful to each other. Generally speaking, moral blame may be attached to either or both spouses not living up to these vows freely and prayerfully entered into, rather than to the divorce decision itself. Of course, when a marriage fails, there are bound to be circumstances where the outlook and hopes of the child may be different from the outlook and intentions of one or both of the parents. For example, where one parent has been seriously and continuously oppressing or neglecting his or her partner but not, directly, the children, the child's point of view may be to regret or resist the divorce of their parents.

However, where one parent behaves extremely unreasonably and unsatisfactorily both to the other parent and to the child, then a divorce might be seen by both the hurt parent and the hurt child to be in the interests of both of them – if for qualitatively different reasons – and in such a case there could be a harmony of acceptance as opposed to parent–child dissonance (latent or overt) over the matter.

Roughly speaking, any real-life situation has to be in a combination of one of the following categories:

- the child, who perceives the divorce as positive or negative;
- the father, who perceives the divorce as positive or negative;
- the mother, who perceives the divorce as positive or negative.

Or to put it more simply, in chart form:

Perception of the consequences of divorce

		By the parent		
		+	+/–	–
By the child	+			
	+/–			
	–			

The chart allows for three principal degrees of the 'felt appropriateness' of divorce, as regards parent and child, the 'readings' of which should be helpful.

In any particular case, a separate chart may be needed for each parent and for each child in relation to each parent. When these are superimposed upon each other the greater the congruence between them the easier it may be to assess the potential for understanding or tensions over a permanent marital break. In practice there will probably most often be a mixture of pluses and minuses, which means that the divorce is at least problematic in some ways.

The chart highlights the fact that divorce is one of the many issues where there may never be a good solution, since every solution puts in the balance a series of pros and cons. In that sense it is vital that the pros and cons of all people involved, particularly the children, are properly heard and dealt with. Some countries in Europe have taken account of this, for example by training judges to listen properly to children. This is an area which good mediation should not miss.

The time of divorce, while supremely appropriate for the parties involved to think calmly and clearly, may be – because of the emotional circumstances – the most difficult time for them to be able to do so. Church members could be gently supportive at such a period by not being hopelessly confused themselves.

Chapter 8

Starting from where we are

When parents divorce, the nature of their changed relationship is not covered by any traditional and accepted term. 'My ex-' or 'your ex-' is a singularly retrospective description. But they are not in the usual sense 'friends' since they have not come together in order just to share a common interest and to enjoy a general affinity and liking. They have been closer than friends: and yet have moved (perhaps quite dramatically and painfully) apart. The changed status of their relationship will be one of legal *dissolution*. Those without children will be free to disappear each from the other into the wider social environment. Those with children do not have that freedom.

The relationship between any divorcing couple, while the divorce is in process, is bound to have the general character of anxiety, tension and confusion, possibly to a significantly high degree. Although it may be that with time, in some circumstances, and with those of certain temperaments, the relationship of a divorced couple could take on something approaching the characteristics of friendship, even of some depth.

While to relate to a former spouse as a mere 'aquaintance' to an onlooker will seem artificial and absurd, it may be helpful to see that, in the short term at least, the relationship between divorcing or divorced parents will be likely to be a more neutral one of 'parenting associates' (a description intended to be very unspecific so far as any 'custody' or 'residence' agreement is concerned). Indeed, such inter-personal neutrality can be seen as a positive point in view of the alternative negative stances and antagonisms which could be adopted –

out of quite natural reaction, defensiveness, or mistrust.

What stands irrevocable is that to their child or children the former husband remains their father and the former wife their mother. But for a child to accept this and at the same time to let go the memory and understanding of their father and mother as husband and wife is heartbreakingly difficult.

Members of Church congregations, who have known and loved a couple with children whose marriage has irreparably failed, have to learn with and from those children in adjusting to the new circumstances.

In reality, divorce is here to stay and the numbers affected appear to be slowly on the increase. Indeed, if the divorce rate in the UK remains at its present level, almost one child in four will experience divorce in the family before reaching the age of sixteen. No formal record is made of the children of re-marrying parents, so the numbers of children who gain a step-parent are unknown. It is estimated that by 2000, only half of all children will spend their childhood with both natural parents. (*Unfinished Business: Children and the Churches*, 1995, section 1.8)

There are four basic attitudes towards to this situation.

On the negative side:

- We should be aware that the culture of post-modernism (where there are no societal norms; what is right is that which is right for me) is not helpful. We should be critical of the tendency to elevate the changing views and feelings of individuals (rather than of couples or communities) to a superior position; this outlook tends to clash with shared understandings, covenanted agreements and accepted certainties which, for example, are intrinsic to and valued in marriage.

- We should take note of the warning of Dr Jack Dominian in his *Passionate and Compassionate Love: A*

Vision for Christian Marriage that 'marriage and the family are the root of society and the Church, and when they are in distress everything else suffers in consequence'.

On the positive side:

● We should take courage from the words of the Chief Rabbi, Dr Jonathan Sacks, who in his 1990 Reith Lectures said that 'The first command in the Bible is to have children, and there is no act we can perform that testifies more lucidly to faith in the future of our world.' He goes on to say: 'The family is a much assaulted, much wounded institution, but it endures: testimony to a sense of covenantal love that can still break through the secular surface of our lives and surprise us by its unexpected and religious strength.'

● We should follow, and commend to others, a Christian action plan for parenting, and for supporting family-sensitive Church children's work and Church youth work, such as that set out below.

Through Church children's work

By children's work, the Church customarily thinks in terms of the under 13s or 14s. Younger children are remarkably sensitive to family and other changes, though they may be helped to be resilient. It is necessary for those in a church congregation with responsibility for children's work, and for leaders in the uniformed organisations, to think of small and very practical ways in which their activities may be especially supportive to those of divorcing or divorced parents. Sometimes this may be simply by arranging for the child to travel with another who is going to the same event.

1 The General Synod Board of Education report *Children in the Way* notes that 'Children in our

churches, as elsewhere, are coping with marriage break-up and separation . . . There will be children and parents needing our support within our congregations and groups' (p.11) and recommends that 'Parishes should consider how they can best support the best traditions of Christian marriage and family life, while affirming their active and sensitive concern and care for all for whom this is not a reality'. (p.24)

2   The Working Party report of the General Synod Board of Education *How Faith Grows* observes under the consideration of 'Faith and the Family' that 'Faith development theory has at least this much in its favour: it make us more aware of, and responsive to, all kinds of change – including the development of our families'. (p.62)

3   The report of the General Synod Board of Education and Board of Mission, *All God's Children?* made the recommendation that every parish should 'examine the demands it is making upon and the support it is giving to Christian parents including support for the Mothers' Union and other similar agencies'. (p.89)

4   The report of The Consultative Group on Ministry among Children, *Unfinished Business*, remarks that 'Unconditional acceptance of single parents, four-parent families, single-sex families and unmarried or common-law parents will pose questions about marriage and divorce, and these cannot be ignored. Yet at the same time the Christian community must be inclusive'. (pp.17, 18) The report goes on to commend a local church where 'There was nowhere suitable for divorced or separated persons to spend time maintaining their relationship with the children to whom they had access. That was until the church decided to use its premises as a contact centre'. (p.66)

Through Church youth work

One of the ways in which young people may feel the knock-on effect of their parents' divorce is a sudden reduction in the standard of living, and a shortage of pocket money. Attendance at a camp or house-party, which could get the young person out of the atmosphere of possible trauma and give them a fresh horizon, may be more than they or the parent with whom they reside could afford – especially if there are other children or young people in the family. A way should be found to make clear to the young person in complete privacy and in a manner that is in no way demeaning that the Church would be prepared to sponsor or subsidise their attendance. The proper and professional maintenance of a Discretionary Fund for such purposes should be put in place.

Youth Leaders should be sensitive to the fact that some young people affected by their parents' divorce simply want to get involved in group or club activities and do not wish to be conscious of or reminded of any problem. Others will value knowing that there is a facility for opening up about personal difficulties – some may prefer an informal situation (individually or in a group), others may respond to the occasional availability of a counsellor who would be willing to see people by appointment. Indeed, for many, the additional anxiety of their parents' subsequent relationships might be uppermost in their minds. The two key factors are, first, that young people's needs will vary – what is right for one will not be right for another (even if they are siblings) – and, second, that the youth activity should concentrate on that activity and not however unintentionally aggravate hurt or difference, or unnecessarily draw attention to it. The best possible thing a Youth Leader can offer is a programme of quality and enjoyable activities in a way which values the young person.

It should be noted that where a young person's parents have divorced, and where one or both have remarried and have started another family of their own, then the 'existing' child may well grow to feel slightly apart from the new family/families and may have a special need for youth settings outside the home.

The teenage years are those in which a young person comes to terms with his or her identity, and therefore any circumstances of background which give rise to difficulty will be likely to be expressed in one way or another. This is technically easier as part of the growing-up process, and among those who know and can informally 'manage' him or her, and signal when he or she is out of order, rather than later in life when such reaction would be perceived as inappropriate and could be damaging or dangerous. Indeed, a safe youth setting could be invaluable for this purpose, but, of course, that could and should never be its primary aim

Recommendation 7 in the General Synod Board of Education report *Youth A Part* states that 'We have a vision of a Church which understands, learns from, and supports young people as they work with issues such as the environment, homelessness, unemployment, family breakdown and depression'. (p.177)

Through Church parents

Church parents whose marriages break up and who form new reconstituted families face a variety of challenges with which they may feel they have a ministry to help others, in due time. As one example, the child of a divorcee whose parent remarries and has another child or more children by their new married partner needs special understanding since not only will he or she be the older child with attention going to a new and younger child, but he or she will become more conscious of ('only') being a half-brother or half-sister to that child and may feel a separateness and lessening of status in comparison. Such a child will need much thoughtful support, time and affection.

Step-parenting as a parent marrying a divorced parent is different in kind from a step-parent marrying a bereaved parent.

In the latter case the step-parent is a substitute for the deceased parent and in some cases this process can be enhanced by adoption. In the former case, i.e. where a step-parent is by marriage to a divorcee, the relationship is of a more temporary and tenuous nature (e.g. 'I'm not your father and I don't want you to regard me as such'), and requires much loving and sensitive understanding and growth in co-operation on both sides in order to work. Not enough attention has been given to the fragility and uncertain nature of this relationship, including the dynamics of how the natural parent might best play his or her role as new spouse and existing parent in this new family situation.

Birth or natural parents, step-parents, single parents, foster parents and godparents must all understand that the Christian vocation to imaginative, loving and patient parenthood involves a willing response to seven factors:

- that in every situation the welfare of the child comes first (Mark 5. 21–4);

- that an atmosphere of love, happiness and understanding in the home is all-important (Mark 10. 13–16);

- that teaching about 'right and wrong' means parents practising, explaining and encouraging behaviour that is safe, constructive and kind (Hosea 11. 1–4);

- that a child is never to be seen as an object but as possessing the sanctity of personhood (Matthew 18. 5, 10);

- that a basic rhythm and order for each day – and using Sunday collectively in a special way – enhances a sense of security and purpose (Luke 4. 16);

- that it is highly responsible for parents to take time out to learn the essentials of child development – and to follow this up as their child grows older (Luke 2. 52);

- that no family can ever be sufficient of itself, but requires the grace of our Lord Jesus Christ and the redemption of Almighty God (John 2. 1, 2).

Appendix A

Prayers

For parents contemplating divorce

ALMIGHTY GOD, we pray for those agonising over the possible prospect of divorce. Comfort them in their distress. Grant them calmness and a clear mind. Assist them to see both the realities and the potential of their alternative futures. Guide them in their exploration of reconciliation. Help them to be considerate of their children and of all others whom their decision would affect. Lead them in being true to themselves in choosing their future path, and in having an overriding desire to live always to your glory; through Jesus Christ, our Lord. Amen.

For parents in the process of divorce

HEAVENLY FATHER, we pray for those who are in the process of divorce: that they may know your presence and your care. Sustain them in their sense of failure. Encourage them in their opportunity to build up a new life. Equip them to be additionally supportive to their children. Assist them to gradually be free of the hold of any deep sense of grievance. Enable them to establish a new relationship of co-operation and concord with the one with whom there was formerly a bond of love; through Jesus Christ, our Lord. Amen.

For parents who are married or who may be divorced

ALMIGHTY GOD
we thank you for the vision of happiness
and promise
of the wedding at Cana in Galilee,
attended by your Son;

grant your special blessing
to all who have taken each other in
holy matrimony:
may their love for each other be enriched,
their life together strengthened,
and their children stimulated and fulfilled;

help your Church to sustain those for whom
the doors of mutuality in marriage
have not remained open:
may they and their children know
the continuing grace of your presence,
and be led in the ways of kindness, peace and
hope;
through Jesus Christ, our Lord.
Amen.

For children experiencing the divorce of their parents

O GOD OUR FATHER, we pray for children and young people who are suffering separation from a loved parent because of the breakdown of marriage, or who are disrupted by the new arrangements of living in two separate places and so feeling that they no longer 'belong' or 'have a home'. Help them to adjust to their new circumstances of living and to enjoy the separate support of both their parents: so that they may be able to continue to be themselves, to respond to the privilege of life, and to share in the community of church, school and neighbourhood; through Jesus Christ, our Lord. Amen.

For a child having to adjust to a reconstituted family

ALMIGHTY GOD, comfort and encourage those children or young people who find that changes in their parents' married life place them in the midst of another and existing family. Help them to come to terms with the challenges this brings. Assist them in their resilience. Encourage them to negotiate positively and to take their place with generosity and goodwill. Grant to the receiving family patience, kindness and understanding towards the young person coming amongst them. We ask this in Christ's name. Amen.

Private prayer for use by a child in lighting a candle in church

LORD JESUS CHRIST, grant that this candle may show my love for my father and my mother, and be a prayer for the light of your love to shine on both of them. Amen.

Private prayer for parents for use by a child or young person

LORD, I thank you for my mother and my father, though I do not always find it easy to understand why they have chosen to live apart; I thank you for their love for me, though I do not really feel quite at the centre of their family any more; [I ask you to bless my brother(s)/my sister(s), and I know they have some unhappy corners in their hearts as I have: but we ask you to make us strong;] I thank you for being the Heavenly Father of each one of us, including our step-relations/any step-relations I/we may have one day; I thank you for tomorrow, and for your comfort and presence with us now and in the future; I pray that you will keep both my parents safe and that we may all be friends; through Jesus Christ, our Lord. Amen.

Appendix B

Useful contacts

For children

Childline   0800 1111
NSPCC   0800 800 500

For parents

Parentline   01702 559 900
Stepfamily   0990 168 388
              (2–5pm, 7–10pm)

Advice and information

Citizen's Advice Bureau
Details of local office: National Association of Citizen's
Advice Bureaux: 0171 833 2181

Family Mediators Association
PO Box 2028, Hove, East Sussex BN3 3HU
Details of local services: 01273 747 750

Solicitors Family Law Association
PO Box 302, Orpington, Kent BR6 8QX
Information solicitors skilled in family work on: 01689 850 227

RELATE
Herbert Gray College, Little Church Street, Rugby,
Warwickshire CV21 3AP
Helpline: 01372 464 100   (Thursdays 12 noon–7pm)
Information about local RELATE services: 01788 573 241

Families Need Fathers
134 Curtain Road, London EC2A 3AR
Information line: 0181 886 0970
Local branches: 0171 613 5060

Appendix C

Useful Books

John Bradford, *Face the Family: Seven Discussion Outlines for Parish Groups*, The Children's Society, 1987.

Monica Cockett and John Tripp, *The Exeter Family Study*, University of Exeter Press, 1996.

Craig Donnelan, *Marriage and Divorce*, Independence, 1996.

Thelma Fisher (ed.), *Family Conciliation within the UK*, Jordan, 1992.

Brynna Kroll, *Chasing Rainbows: Children, Divorce and Loss*, Russell House Publishing, 1994.

Judith S. Wallerstein and Sandra Blakeslee, *Second Chances: Men, Women and Children – A Decade after Divorce*, Bantam Press, 1989.

Sue Walrond-Skinner, *Family Matters: The Pastoral Care of Personal Relationships*, SPCK, 1995.

Robert Warren, *Divorce and Remarriage: Policy Options and Pastoral Guidelines for Church Leaders*, Grove Booklets, 1992.

Two useful books for younger children:

'Althea', *My Two Families*, A. & C. Black, 1996.

Ginny Perkins, *Remembering my Brother*, A. & C. Black, 1996.

Appendix D

References

Archbishop of Canterbury's Working Group on Divorce, *Putting Asunder*, SPCK, 1966.

O. Ayalon and A. Flasher, *Chain Reaction: Children and Divorce*, Jessica Kingsley Press, 1993.

L. Burghes, *Lone Parenthood and Family Disruption*, Family Policy Studies Centre, 1994.

G. Davis and M. Murch, *Grounds for Divorce*, Clarendon Press, 1988.

Jack Dominian, *Passionate and Compassionate Love: A Vision for Christian Marriage*, DLT, 1991.

General Synod Board for Social Responsibility, *Something to Celebrate: Valuing Families in Church and Society*, Church House Publishing, 1995.

General Synod Board of Education, *Children in the Way*, National Society/Church House Publishing, 1988.

General Synod Board of Education, *How Faith Grows*, National Society/Church House Publishing, 1991.

General Synod Board of Education, *Youth A Part*, National Society/Church House Publishing, 1996.

General Synod Board of Education and Board of Mission, *All God's Children*, National Society/Church House Publishing, 1991.

General Synod of the Church of England, *Divorce Law Reform: The Government's Proposals*, 1994.

Law Commission, *The Field of Choice*, HMSO, 1966 [CMMD 3123].

Methodist Church Division of Social Responsibility, *Preparing for Christian Marriage*, Methodist Publishing House, 1996.

Diana Murrie and Steve Pearce, *Children and Holy Communion*, National Society/Church House Publishing, 1997.

Occasional Celebrations of the Anglican Church of Canada, Anglican Book Centre, Toronto, 1992.

Report of Consultative Group on Ministry among Children, *Unfinished Business: Children and the Churches*, CCBI Publications, 1995.

Anne Tanner, *Treasures of Darkness*, Anglican Book Centre, Toronto, 1990.

Stefan Venistendael, *Growth in the Muddle of Life – Resilience: Building on People's Strengths*, International Catholic Child Bureau, 2nd edn, 1996.

Judith Wallerstein and Joan B. Kelly, *Surviving the Break-up: How Children and Parents Cope with Divorce*, Grant MacIntyre, 1980.

John H. Westerhoff III and William H. Willimon, *Liturgy and Learning through the Life Cycle*, Seabury Press, 1980.